Moon Juice

Poems by Kate Wakeling

With illustrations by Elīna Brasliņa

THE EMMA PRESS
CHILDREN'S BOOKS

For Dad

THE EMMA PRESS

First published in Great Britain in 2016
by the Emma Press Ltd

Reprinted in 2017

ISBN 978-1-910139-49-3

A CIP catalogue record of this book
is available from the British Library.

Printed and bound in Great Britain
by TJ International, Padstow.

The Emma Press
theemmapress.com
queries@theemmapress.com
Jewellery Quarter, Birmingham, UK

MOON JUICE

PRAISE FOR *MOON JUICE*

'This clever, funny, inspiring poetry collection [...] is a children's debut by a poet for adults, full of rich ideas and roll-round the tongue sounds that demand to be read aloud.'
The Sunday Times

'This collection takes a delight in the power of language, imagination and the white space that surrounds each poem. This is a confident and versatile debut from a welcome new voice in children's poetry.' Rachel Rooney, author of *The Language of Cat*

'A brilliant collection packed with intriguing characters, myth and mind-popping ideas from a fresh, original voice.'
Joseph Coelho, author of *Werewolf Club Rules*

This collection of twenty-five poems is richly varied in subject matter, tone and style, mixing silliness with subtle storytelling and childhood realities with interplanetary vistas, whilst also creating space to give voice to big and difficult emotions at the same time as making us laugh a little mischievously as we turn the pages.' Zoe Toft, *Playing By The Book*

---

bo
ary
v.cu
rie

Contents

MOON JUICE BONUS BITS

Moon Juice

New Moon

Moon is
silver sliver.

Moon is
clipped cup
from which to sip
a first drop
of freshly-pressed
moon juice.

Moon is
somersaulting C
in the best moon font.

Moon is fickle flickerer.

Moon is
new lunar lantern
to track a star or two.

But mostly,
moon is
shy to meet
once more
that
old old
sky.

Skig the Warrior

Skig the warrior was more of a worrier.

He didn't want to spear deer
or pillage villages
or hoot and toot when the crew looted somewhere new.

He'd rather play Scrabble than join the rack and rabble.

Yep, Skig was in no hurry to be a warrior.
It only made him worry (and sorrier).

Bad Moods

Bad Moods wear weird shoes.
Bad Moods wear weird shoes
covered in unexpected fleecy fluff
that mean Bad Moods can creep up on you
like spiders or tigers or a daddy longlegs with silent stilts.

Bad Moods wear weird shoes
that mean Bad Moods can creep up on you
and then, when you're alone

and a Bad Mood has slunk into that curl of muscle and bone
that is your EARHOLE,
the Bad Mood will tear off its weird shoes
and underneath is wearing ENORMOUS CLOD-
  HOPPERS
so it can bang around
even though only you can hear it
(you hope).

Bad Moods gobble grins for breakfast
then spit them out as mangled toads.

Bad Moods smell like bat droppings, old eggs and damp,
  cross dogs.
Bad Moods can't finish even their own sentences because—
Bad Moods are just so—
Bad Moods have you in their—
Bad Moods won't—

Bad Moods wear weird shoes
because *that* is what Bad Moods do.

Comet

(To be read as quickly as possible, in as few breaths as you can manage.)

I'm a spinning, winning, tripping, zipping, super-sonic ice queen:
see my moon zoom, clock my rocket, watch me splutter tricksy space-steam.

I'm the dust bomb, I'm the freeze sneeze, I'm the top galactic jockey
made (they think) of gas and ice and mystery bits of something rocky.

Oh I sting a sherbet orbit, running rings round star or planet;
should I shoot too near the sun, my tail hots up: *ouch – OUCH – please fan it!*

And I'm told I hold the answer to the galaxy's top question:
that my middle's made of history (no surprise I've indigestion)

but for now I sprint and skid and whisk and bolt and belt and bomb it;
I'm that hell-for-leather, lunging, plunging, helter-skelter COMET.

Instruments of Use

You can do all sorts with a musical instrument, if
  you listen hard enough:

You can call a friend with a xylophone.
You can catch a fish with a clarinet.
You can build a skeleton with a trombone.
You can cover a street with an electric guitar.

And, if your guinea-pig has recently taken a turn for
  the worse,
you're very welcome to borrow my trumpet.

My Ghost Sister

I see her
>though nobody else can.

Her nose is the same as mine,

but she's taller – thinner too:

I think I could throw a ball right through her.

I see her in the blue gleam of computer screens

and in the   r

    a

    i

    n

       on windowpanes.

Sometimes she sits in my room at night,

        her pale hands still,

      her misty breath quiet as a   cloud.

            Her ghost bones glow.

        A while ago I told Dad

about my ghost sister

and he looked tired and grey.

He said: *Good to know she's about.*

           Best keep it quiet though.

So I do.

But when I'm stuck or hurt or low,

I know she's close

with her softest sister-ghost hello,

for we're not ready,
not just yet,

to say

goodbye.

Hair Piece

A while back, I wanted hair that was curly so badly that I got a thing called a perm (which stands for 'permanent wave'). But the lady I paid to primp my hair into a perm put too much of the curly chemical on and after not long my hair felt like a scorched hayfield and started to snap off. So for a while I called myself "Tufty". Until other people started to call me "Tufty" too. And I told all this to my friend (sadly not called Shirley) who had hair that was curly but wished fate had dealt her hair that was straight, so she ironed it flat with tongs which also burnt it to a crisp and made it snap off. And amid these wrongs we could both see there was something worth learning. But it was difficult to concentrate on this something, what with the smell of all that burning.

Jungle Cat

I lived for a while in a village in Indonesia.
After many nights hearing strange noises coming from the
ceiling, I found out I was sharing the house with a jungle
cat. Jungle cats are larger than ordinary cats with long legs
and an extra tuft of fur on each ear.

They told me
you live in my roof,
jungle cat.

Fire-eyed
trick-tailed
sleep thief.

You rumble the night
with your claw dance,
your tooth song.

I hear you yowl and pounce
and hiss and purr.

You scratch my sleep.

You creep across my cat naps.

Years later,
I find you still roaming my roof,
a wild thing
grinning
in the black night.

Rich Pickings

A scab's your own personal pie crust,
its insides cooked up nice and pink.
Make sure not to fiddle before it is done:
an itch tells you it's on the brink.

Yes, a scab's your own personal pie crust,
and I favour a filling of knee.
But don't think that this morsel's for sharing:
this pie crust belongs just to me.

THE INSTRUCTIONS

1. How to spot THE INSTRUCTIONS

THE INSTRUCTIONS come in all shapes and sizes. They are often found in and around:

* *Tall buildings with statues of lions outside*
* *Faces with an angry expression*
* *Faces with a smile seen only in the mouth but (crucially) not in the eyes*

2. The other instructions

There are plenty of *other* sorts of instructions, which can of course be useful.
For example:

* *Try not to insert any part of your body into this pond: it contains an irritated crocodile*
* *For best results, keep both eyes open while landing this lopsided helicopter*
* *Do not under any circumstances eat the angry man's sandwich*

3. What THE INSTRUCTIONS want

You see, THE INSTRUCTIONS aren't here to help you.
They want to help someone or something else.
THE INSTRUCTIONS say things like:

> *No one's ever done THAT before: it CAN'T be a good idea.*
> *Please do the SAME thing as all those OTHER people over THERE.*
> *Hear that person talking in the PARTICULARLY loud voice? They must DEFINITELY be RIGHT.*

4. If you follow THE INSTRUCTIONS

If you follow THE INSTRUCTIONS it is unlikely anyone will ever be very cross with you.
If you follow THE INSTRUCTIONS you are guaranteed to feel neat and tidy (but also a little short of breath).

5. If you do not follow THE INSTRUCTIONS

You will likely face some tricky moments. Apologies for this.
However, there is also a good chance that something

strangeexcitingremarkableunexpectedslightly-
frighteningbutbrightlycoloured

will happen.

6. The choice

is yours.

Hamster Man

He's one-half hamster, one-half man,
he rides around in a caravan.

He's six-foot tall with furry ears
(and 107 in hamster years).

He answers the phone with three sharp squeaks.
He stores ham sandwiches in his cheeks.

His wits are as sharp as his two front teeth
but he turns to mush when scratched beneath

his chin. Oh Hamster Man's the real deal,
running all night on his giant wheel.

He's one of a kind, there ain't no clan
of rodent men, just Hamster Man.

Night Journey

When it's like this,

when mum is driving
and everyone is quiet,
heads toppling with sleep,
and the motorway is a dizzy black
slicked with lights,

when it's like this,

the car is not a mile machine.

It is a thought machine.

New thoughts fizz from nowhere.

New thoughts tick and gleam,
find strange shapes,
strange colours,
build things,
grow wings.

New thoughts sizzle out into the dark.

Old thoughts find new homes,
new roads
or
pop like bubbles.

Worries go slow mo,
fade to grey
and vanish.

Because the car is not a mile machine.

It is a thought machine.

Thief

He'll steal your keys,
he'll steal your cheese,
he'll steal your dreams from out your earhole.

He'll steal your spoons,
he'll steal your tunes,
he'll steal the ball and score an own goal.

He'll steal your van,
he'll steal your plan,
he'll steal the goldfish *and* the fish bowl.

And if I give him just a moment in this steal-a-minute age,
he'll steal the very thing I'm writing here clean off the

Little-Known Facts

In secret, children can turn lightbulbs on and off with just their eyebrows.

When a child sneezes, the nearest adult briefly loses all reception on their mobile phone.

Left unwashed, children's feet smell of perfectly-cooked spaghetti.

You can predict the next day's weather based on how tightly a child's hair curls after a bath (extra curly = sunshine).

Behind children's left ears grow tiny cacti which yield delicious juice every summer.

Children can see through brick walls of up to 15cm thick, if the thing on the other side is definitely worth looking at.

When a child jumps up and down, fish in the nearest pond rise to the surface and blow a celebratory stream of bubbles.

Children can set up a reliable internet connection in any location using a pigeon and two drinking straws.

Children are able to smell a lie being told from 180 metres away.

I Found a Dinosaur
Under the Shed

I found a dinosaur under the shed.
A tiny one, no taller than my shin.

He had yellow blinking eyes
and leathery wings.

He crouched in the dark,
trembling.

I fed him popcorn and caterpillars,
built him a nest from twigs and an old jumper.

As the weeks passed, he began to hop at my ankles,
squawking his dinosaur cry
when I scratched his head.

I'd creep out of the house in the moonlight
to find him curled in his nest,
purring like a cat.

I liked his scaly skin
that was as old as it was new.

I liked that he hissed at the spiders
but not at me.

I saw he was getting bigger,
that the space under the shed was too small,
his nest too narrow.

When I sat beside him I found
he was now as tall as my shoulder.

His teeth shone.

At night I heard him stride around the garden,
beating his wings and trying to fly.

Soon he could only just fit in his nest,
his dinosaur tail curled round him,
his nose poked up against the wood of the shed.

I found him more popcorn,
more caterpillars,

but we both heard his stomach growl.

I asked him not to leave.

The last time I saw him
he tried to keep his wide mouth closed,
to keep his jaw from glinting.

I watched his long claws twitch.

The next day I found his footprints in the mud:
a mark,
a mark,
then nothing.

Machine

My machine, my machine, meet my fine new machine:
note its clever design, see its marvellous sheen.
Now, I hear it's the first with this all-improved screen
that can function as friend, fridge, page, pet and latrine.*

Oh how neatly it fits in your bag, hand or brain;
it can film all your daydreams and switch off the rain;
it puts time in reverse if you're missing a train –
and when troubled, just switch all its settings to SANE.

For this thing was designed by a top engineer
to delete chance and boredom and wonder and fear,
so if feeling fed up with the hour, day or year,
simply turn to the menu and click <disappear>

A latrine is an old-fashioned name for a toilet.

The Serpent and the Turtle
(or: A Very Balinese Beginning)

———————

Now, if you lie an ear to the earth
you'll hear it had many beginnings:
beginnings that began with birds or bridges or ice or eggs
or *you name it*, someone will tell you a story that starts with it.

So, here is one such beginning to the world
and it is told to us from the small, green island of Bali
and it is certainly a good'un.
Or, as a Balinese person might say: *eyyyyy, bechik–bechik.*

At this beginning of the world
there was not too much of anything
(as is often the case).
There was only a flat, single nothing which was all at once the
longest-shortest-clearest-cloudiest-sweetest-sourest-
　nothingest
nothing that ever there was.
Or rather, wasn't.

And in the middle of this nothing
there lived a snakey, serpenty slitherer called Antaboga.
(You can rhyme Antaboga with *Rant! A frog jar!*
but I suggest you don't.)
Antaboga the serpent had a slipping, sliding rainbow belly
and he was as long as a story with no end
but twice as lonely.

One morning, Antaboga decided it was about time
there was less *nothing*
and more *something*.

So this is what he did:
Antaboga closed his cool, black eyes
and fell into a long, low snooze
that bid his blood to doze in his veins,
while deep inside his green and serpenty brains
he began to dream of a

        t   u   r   t   l   e

a turtle so huge, so high, so mind-janglingly enormous
that even the tiniest tooth
at the back of the turtle's great green mouth
was twenty-two times taller
than the mightiest mountain you could imagine.

And just like that, the turtle appeared,
for this is how things were done in those days.

The turtle's name was Bedwang,
(which is said just as you want to say it)
and Bedwang (correct!) also agreed it was about time
there was less *nothing*
and more *something*.

Better yet, Bedwang the turtle had an idea.

He realised his huge green shell
was the perfect place to put
islands and oceans and songs and gongs and people and
  pineapples,
by which Bedwang meant

    e   v   e   r   y   t   h   i   n   g

and no sooner had Bedwang the turtle begun to imagine
islands and oceans and songs and gongs and people and
  pineapples
balanced on his shell,
then just like that, they appeared,
for this is how things were done in those days.

There was, however, a problem.

When everything had settled on Bedwang's back,
Bedwang found he had a fidget in his front left foot
and try as he might not to fidget,

                                        fidget he did,
and the instant he twitched
so the world above him twitched
and the ocean bellowed and the ground trembled
and Bedwang saw that he'd better be careful,
for no one wants bellows or trembles like those.
But as everybody knows,
a fidget can be tricky to refuse.

And so it came to pass
that Antaboga the serpent and Bedwang the turtle
had made the world and given it a home,
and while Bedwang slept and twitched and twitched and slept
(which meant the world on his back
slept and twitched and twitched and slept),
still Antaboga and his rainbow belly drifted on beyond
  the skies,
as long as a story with no end
but now twice as cheerful.

And that, dear reader,
is how this particular beginning
began.

The Spy Café

The Spy Café's a peculiar place.

The sign on the door only ever says CLOSED.

They keep the lighting way down low
and the menu's written in invisible ink.

The special of the day is usually Spy Pie
(with the filling kept TOP SECRET).

No one has *ever seen the cook*.

The spies don't say much,
preferring to ink coded messages on napkins
and leave them casually on the other spies' plates.

The waiters wear wigs and dark glasses.

They mutter things like

>   *the badger is in the hole*

to nobody in particular.

I'd suggest we meet for a cup of tea
but the Spy Café can be difficult to find.

Very difficult to find.

Very, very difficult to find.

Telescope

O
telescOpe
telescOpe
shOw me
hOw
the mOon
glOws
shOw me

whO
the wOrld
knOws
shOw me
the prOgress
Of
thOse
skybOund
bOdies
frOm the
PlOugh to
cOld
Old
PlutO
shOw me
telescOpe
shOw me
the wOnders
that revOlve
beyOnd
yOur
cOol
pOlished
O

The Demon Mouth

One day, the Demon Mouth came to the door.

They wouldn't let it in
(would *you* let it in?)
but the Demon Mouth ate the lock.

The Demon Mouth rumbled into the kitchen
and ate the crisps and carrots and cakes.

It ate the bread, the beans, the beef.

And then it ate the fridge.

They shouted and scowled
until the Demon Mouth ate the words out of their mouths.

They tried to catch it
but the Demon Mouth ate the sprint out of their heels.

They didn't know what to do.
They didn't know what to do.

And then
it tried to eat the dog
and they knew they had to do *something*.

So they called the medicine woman
and asked her to stop the Demon Mouth.

She said *this mouth just needs feeding.*

Everyone looked at her like the Demon Mouth
had eaten the brains out of her skull.

She said *I promise you, this mouth just needs feeding.*

No one believed her:
the Demon Mouth had eaten everything it could find
but the medicine woman shook her head
and said
that isn't the same as being FED.

Still no one believed her
but they thought they might as well try.

So they found a biscuit
and gently gave it to the Demon Mouth
who in a demon blur gobbled it down
then gave something like a purr.

So they gave it another biscuit
and a banana
and a bowl of rice and peas
and were just pondering dessert

when the Demon Mouth let out a floor-rattling burp.

They gave it radishes
and raisins
and a bag of onion rings
and the Demon Mouth began to grin.

And when they took out a toffee pudding
the Demon Mouth paused,
then closed
and, just like that,
crept gently off.

And no one could believe
the Demon Mouth had gone
(just like that)
on being *fed*

but it did.

And the medicine woman smiled
and walked quietly away,
saying
that mouth just needed feeding
that mouth just needed feeding.

Dodo

I'm sorry, Dodo,
that you're now the logo
for the no-go
animal, that you had to pogo
off the planet as people were so slow
to forgo
hunting your excellent beak. I'm oh so
sorry that you're now the No. 1 no-show,
Dodo.

Spirit Bridge

In Bali, many believe rivers and ravines to be the home of leyak (lay-ack). Leyak are fierce witches who can transform themselves into other beings such as dogs, monkeys, heads without bodies and mysterious, moving lights.

In the deep green,
in the heat of the gloom,
a leyak creeps across its selves:

       fish,

    beetle,

         monkey,

            bat,

               a lone and drifting skull.

The bridge creaks.

A footstep.

Somebody comes.

Choosing a shape,
the leyak slips
to the water's edge.

The footstep waits.

The leyak waits.

A trembling light
rises from the bank
to blink beneath the bridge.

For one white-shot moment
the trees
the path
the water
all burn in the quick cold light of the leyak.

A gasp.

A face.

A reaching hand.

Darkness returns,
the quiet
unsettled
only by the muffled
whisper
of the river
scrambling
below.

Shadow Boy

Shadow boy's as shy as they come.
Dark as charcoal,
thin as air,
he tiptoes at the heels of his friends,
or lingers
patiently
under trees,
behind the wall,
at the base of a lamppost,
hoping to catch
a friendly foot.

Shadow boy's as shy as they come.
He tries his best
to brave the dark,
daring
to grow taller
and taller
as the sun sets.
But come the night,
shy shadow boy can only fade
then wait
until the bright dawn breaks.

Rita the Pirate

Let me warn you of Rita, the pirate supreme:
she'll grab all your gold with an ear-splitting scream.

What she lacks in back teeth she makes up in back bone;
with her horrible stare, she turns grown men to stone.

She steers her great boat with her crooked quick wits
and a cackling crew of rogues, cheats and misfits.

She'll go head-to-head with a hammerhead shark
for it's clear that her bite's just as bad as her bark.

Yes, Rita's old soul is as cold as they come,
there's little feared more than the sound of her drum.

And they say Rita won't touch a toe on dry land
but I'd keep your door locked (and the breadknife to hand).

The Ten Dark Toes at the Bottom of the Bed

I know they belong to me,
those toes,
those ten dark toes,
and yet
they have a certain look about them,
twitching in the shadows
laying their plans,
all overseen by the big toe chiefs
(though it's the little ones I trust the least).

I pull the duvet up,
take a deep breath

and cross my fingers.

This be the scale

(Listen closely.)

1. Sound of Jupiter's stomach rumbling.

2. All the world's thunder heard as one tremendous roar.

3. Thud of large dinosaur chasing its own tail.

4. Low hum of double-decker buses, night-time worry and unlit cellars.

5. Bark of large to medium-sized dog.

6. Rasp of someone in the next room scraping the black bits off a piece of burnt toast.

7. Gasp of this same someone on discovering the toast was burnt in the first place.

8. Bark of considerably smaller dog.

9. Collective hiss heard as classroom faces unanswerable exam question.

10. One-note shriek of fanged monkeys, unripe grapefruits and all neon lights.

11. Top-notch ping of new moons and the first hint of sunshine on a birthday morning.

12.

Moon Juice
BONUS BITS

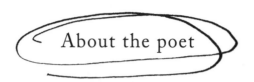

About the poet

Kate Wakeling is a poet and ethnomusicologist. Her poetry has appeared in magazines and anthologies including *Oxford Poetry*, the *Guardian* and *The Forward Book of Poetry 2016*, and a pamphlet of her poetry for adults, *The Rainbow Faults*, is published by The Rialto. *Moon Juice* is her first poetry collection for children.

Kate is writer-in-residence with Aurora Orchestra and writes for TROUPE concerts. Her scripts and stories for family audiences have featured at the Melbourne Festival, the bOing! Festival and on BBC Radio 3.

Kate studied music at Cambridge University and holds a PhD in Balinese gamelan music from the School of Oriental & African Studies. She lives in Oxford with her husband and son.

Visit Kate's website here: www.katewakeling.co.uk

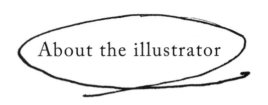

About the illustrator

Elīna Brasliņa studied Printmaking and Graphic Arts at the Art Academy of Latvia. Since 2014 she has illustrated ten titles, including *Moon Juice*, which is her international debut.

She has received a number of nominations in Latvia and was twice awarded the Zelta Ābele (Golden Apple Tree) National Prize for Book Art.

You can visit Elīna's website and see more of her illustrations here: www.elinabraslina.com

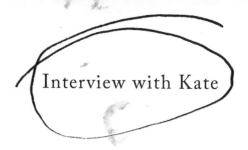

Interview with Kate

When did you start writing poems?

I think when I was about 8 or 9.

Do you remember what the first poem you wrote was about?

I'm not sure it was the very first, but when I was small I was in a school play and when it ended I felt completely miserable. I wrote a poem to try to catch and fix the magical sensation of being in this play.

I can't remember what the poem said but I do remember how writing it immediately made me feel better – like there was a way after all to hold on to this good feeling.

What was your favourite subject at school?

Art! I wasn't especially good at it but I loved the feeling of being able to get on with your own drawing or painting (or whatever it was) alongside other people – sometimes chatting, sometimes being quiet. The hum of a happy school art room is surely one of the best sounds ever.

Which is your favourite illustration in this book?

I absolutely love all of Elīna's illustrations! But if I had to choose one, I'd pick the Demon Mouth being fed by the medicine woman. I only had a hazy image of what these characters might actually look like until I saw Elīna's illustration and BANG, she knew exactly who they were.

What advice would you give someone who hadn't written a poem before but might like to?

Firstly, go for it. A poem can be whatever you want it to be: long, short, sad, funny, something in-between (as many of the best ones are). I'd say when you begin a poem, first be as wild and messy and free as you can – write as though your pen or keyboard is on fire! – then change hats and become as patient and picky as possible.

For me, writing a poem is half about letting your imagination zoom and half about being furiously fussy to make sure every word counts. Lastly, try not to choose words just for what they mean but explore how they sound too. If you let these sounds lead the way, all sorts of unexpected and excellent things will happen to your poem.

———————

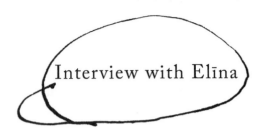

Interview with Elīna

How did you become an illustrator?

Literature and art are the two great loves of my life. Before entering the Art Academy I studied French at the University of Latvia and dreamed of translating fiction, but my artistic ambition caught up with me.

Illustrating books seemed like a way to combine these two passions – reading and drawing. And, of course, I owe a lot to my teachers for steering me in the right direction and introducing me to publishers.

What advice would you give someone who wants to be an illustrator?

Three words: observe, draw and draw again. It's great to exercise your imagination, but you can pick up a lot of ideas just by keeping your eyes and ears open.

And never stop searching for new techniques, new subject matter, new ways of challenging yourself. But, most of all, love what you do.

What's your favourite poem in this book?

It's really hard to choose just one, because I had so much fun illustrating all of them.

But one of my absolute favourites is 'Rich Pickings' – I imagine some readers finding it hard to stomach, but I think it's hilarious, daring in its honesty and very relatable.

What projects are you working on at the moment?

I'm currently working for Atom Art, an independent Latvian animation studio, creating character and background designs for an animated feature film called *Jacob, Mimmi and the Talking Dogs,* which will be released in 2018.

I'm also illustrating a children's novel about art detectives and a picture book about a dog who's looking for ways to overcome sadness.

What's your favourite thing to draw?

Large crowds – it's easy to slip in details, even devious and transgressive ones, and I think readers enjoy crowd scenes, especially kids, because they can revisit them and always find something they hadn't noticed before.

———

Thank you for answering all our questions, Kate and Elīna!

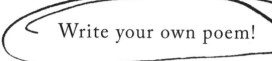

Write your own poem!

Fancy writing your own poem and maybe illustrating it afterwards? Kate's editor Rachel Piercey has come up with some ideas to get you started.

 What might be found in **moon juice** (p. 1)? Write a list poem of ingredients, describing each of them in detail like in a recipe.

Poor old **Skig the warrior** (p. 3) isn't very well-suited to his job. Jot down some other jobs and the personal qualities that would make someone bad at them, then choose your favourite and write a poem.

(81)

Kate imagines various things you could do with a **musical instrument** (p. 11). Think of a room in the house and make a list of some of the items that belong there (e.g. kettle, toaster, cutlery drawer…).

Then select four or five and imagine what else you could use them for – the stranger the better!

Kate has chosen to lay out her poem so every line except the last two starts with 'You'. How will you structure your poem? Will you have some kind of pattern?

Remember the one and only **Hamster Man** (p. 27)? Create your own unique animal-human mash up!

Try to use several of the five senses to draw the reader into the world of your poem – for example, what does your animal-human sound and smell like?

In '**Little-Known Facts**' (p. 34), Kate has let her imagination run wild! Have fun creating your own little-known facts – they might be about children, a particular animal, a particular place, or anything that takes your fancy.

Some of Kate's poems, like 'I Found a Dinosaur Under the Shed' (p. 36), 'The Serpent and the Turtle' (p. 42) and 'The Demon Mouth' (p. 53), tell a story.

Read these poems again and see how Kate has picked out particular actions and details to move the story along. Then write your own story-poem about one of the characters in *Moon Juice*, or another of your favourite books.

Write a poem entitled 'The Further Adventures of **Rita the Pirate**'.

ABOUT THE EMMA PRESS

small press, big dreams

The Emma Press is a Birmingham-based publishing house which makes books for adults and children. Emma Wright set it up in 2012 and works on all the books with her best friend from school, Rachel Piercey.

Emma Press books are starting to win prizes, including the Poetry Book Society Pamphlet Choice Award and the Saboteur Award for Best Collaborative Work. Having been shortlisted for the Michael Marks Award for Poetry Pamphlet Publishers in both 2014 and 2015, the Emma Press finally won it in 2016 (hurray!).

Falling Out of the Sky: Poems about Myths and Monsters, the first Emma Press poetry book for children, was shortlisted for the 2016 CLiPPA, run by the Centre for Literacy in Primary Education. *Moon Juice* won the CLiPPA in 2017.

You can find out more about the Emma Press and buy books directly from us here:
theemmapress.com

Also from the Emma Press

The Noisy Classroom
by Ieva Flamingo

Illustrated by Vivianna Maria Staņislavska & Translated by Žanete
Vēvere Pasqualini, Sara Smith and Richard O'Brien
RRP £8.50 / ISBN 978-1-910139-82-0 / Aimed at children aged 8+

It isn't easy being a kid — especially not in the noisiest class in
the school. Some days, you struggle with algebra, or too much
homework. Sometimes, one of your fellow pupils just won't
SHUT UP. When the class feels like a many-headed dragon,
how can you find a place for yourself? Would you feel less
lonely if you could smuggle a cat in? And when your parents
are fighting, don't you find yourself looking into other people's
windows on the walk back home?

Also from the Emma Press

Watcher of the Skies
Poems about space and aliens

Edited by Rachel Piercey and Emma Wright
With science facts by astrophysicist Rachel Cochrane
RRP £8.50 / ISBN 978-1-910139-43-1 / Aimed at children aged 8+

How big is the universe? Are there dogs in space? What
if your friend – or your granddad – was an alien? Join
the poets in wondering in *Watcher of the Skies*, a sparkling
collection of poems about the outermost possibilities of
space, life and our imaginations.

*'This is a book which truly has something for everyone. [...]
This is a collection that deserves a place on the shelves of any
young science enthusiasts and which we're sure will also bring
adult readers plenty to discover and marvel at.'*
One Giant Read

Also from the Emma Press

FALLING OUT OF THE SKY
POEMS ABOUT MYTHS & MONSTERS

Edited by Rachel Piercey and Emma Wright

RRP £8.50 / ISBN 978-1-910139-18-9 / Aimed at children aged 9+

Who helped Theseus defeat the Minotaur? How did
Antaboga the serpent create the world? Why was Arachne
turned into a spider? And what did Loki do to bring about
the end of the world? Find out in *Falling Out of the Sky*,
a treasury of poems about myths and legends by twenty
modern poets. Featuring mischievous gods, ferocious
villains, witches, wizards and monsters – who might not all
be as monstrous as the stories say...

**Shortlisted for the 2016 CLiPPA, the Centre for Literacy in
Primary Education's award for children's poetry books**

*'An exciting collection that challenges in a way few
anthologies for children do.'* The 2016 CLiPPA judges